GW01159483

THE DOWRY OF
THE VIRGIN

THE DOWRY OF THE VIRGIN

A Book of Poems

"And if a man entices a maid that is not betrothed,
And lie with her; he shall surely endow her to be his wife.
If her father utterly refuses to give her unto him,
He shall pay money according to the Dowry of Virgins"

EXODUS 22 Verses 16-17
Authorized King James Version.

ONYEALI KINGSLEY

Strategic Book Publishing and Rights Co.

Copyright © 2020 Onyeali Kingsley. All rights reserved.

No part of this book may be reproduced or transmitted in any form or by any means, graphic, electronic, or mechanical, including photocopying, recording, taping, or by any information storage retrieval system, without the permission, in writing, of the publisher. For more information, email support@sbpra.net, Attention: Subsidiary Rights.

Strategic Book Publishing & Rights Co., LLC
USA | Singapore
www.sbpra.net

For information about special discounts for bulk purchases, please contact Strategic Book Publishing and Rights Co. Special Sales, at bookorder@sbpra.net.

ISBN: 978-1-950860-11-1

ACKNOWLEDGEMENTS

I wish to express my heartfelt gratitude to all those who read my first few set of poems and encouraged me to write more and have them published for wider readership.

I appreciate the positive role played by Professor Nkem Okoh, Head of Department, Department of English Studies, University of Port Harcourt, Port Harcourt, who guided me from the manuscript to the publication stages of this book.

I will also appreciate Dr. Margaret Fafa Nutsukpo of Department of English Studies, University of Port Harcourt, Port Harcourt, who despite her tight schedule, still volunteered her time to review the work and also wrote a glowing Foreword for the book.

My appreciation also goes to my dear wife, **Mercy** Odinakachi, and my beautiful daughter and a champion in her own right, Chimamanda Tiffany-Royal, who inspired me in more ways than one during the collection and publication of this book.

Finally, I am deeply indebted to **God Almighty** for creating me and sowing the seed of poetry in me and giving me the wherewithal to hone it and have my poems published in a book for wider readership. By strength shall no man prevail, but by the Spirit of God Almighty.

FOREWORD

Mr. Kingsley Onyeali is a budding poet who is a lawyer by profession. Although he currently resides in Port Harcourt, Rivers State, Onyeali is a native of Imo State, Nigeria.

Onyeali's first collection of thirty poems, titled The Dowry of the Virgin revolves around social, religious and political themes.

Under these themes are various sub-themes such as disillusionment, friendship and love, socio-political and economic exploitation, and hope for a better tomorrow.

The tone of this collection is set by the opening poem, "Unpatriotic Communiqué", which reveals the poet's disillusionment with the shortcomings of his homeland:

> I hate this place I was found in
> I wish I were found
> Strolling down to somewhere
> And skyscrapers, penthouses
> Fix their eyes upon me

The persona's evident desire for a more advanced environment, with better opportunities than what pertains in his homeland, is evident in the lines above. At the same time, there is an underlying sense of guilt for his dissatisfaction with his lot.

In "Omnipotent Creed" the poet leans towards the religious, highlighting the theme of salvation through mercy and forgiveness. The persona cries:

> Falling from grace
> Into miry clay
> Your outstretched hands
> Lift me up
> To your bosom
> Like an apple of your dear heart
> I see love
> That washes me clean

The religious theme is also evident in poems such as "The Preacher" and "Trees and Flowers".

In "Have You Seen Who My Heart Ticks For?", however, the theme of love and friendship resonates:

> Behold! She is like a tender leaf
> Hidden on the slopes
> Of the Northern hills
> And a prayer
> That calms down
> My frayed nerves

And beats small
My mountain rage

This woman, who has a special place in the heart of the persona, is also identified as his "queen" who sits "beside [his] royal stool".

A good number of the poems are commentaries that speak against societal and political injustice. Poems such as "The Kidnappers", "African Child Witches", "The Blues of Gaza" and "Supreme Lies" are good examples here. In "The Blues of Gaza", the speaking voice rings with conviction that a fallen Gaza shall rise again:

Gaza shall rise! Gaza shall rise!
Like a leaf of the living branch in the
    spring time
By the hands of his fathers of the latter
    rain.

In "The Supreme Lies", however, the voice, faced with the injustice and corruption in the land, laments:

Behold the hope of mankind dies!
When the fountain of justice dries
The lip of the nation cries
Under the weight of supreme lies...

Some of the most striking poems in the collection are those that highlight the poet's concern about the Niger Delta region of Nigeria – the degradation of the land as a result of persistent oil exploration by multinational oil companies (in partnership with the Nigerian government), with dire consequences for the "owners" of the land. In verse two of the title poem, "The Dowry of the Virgin", the persona decries this ugly trend which robs the natives of the land of, not only their means of livelihood, but also the benefits accrued from the exploitation of their oil-rich land, the Niger Delta:

> They take away everything foretold
> Her precious stones, pearls and gold
> Hidden deep beneath her ebony skin
> All gone like vapour in the tropical sun
> Up they stand a long way off her shores
> So rich with the wealth of Delta's stores
> While she is left in the ashes of ruin
> Like an orphan child in a blistering cold

Other poems that highlight this dire situation are "The sail of Our Twisted Masters", and "Ashes of Ruins".

I find each of the poems in this collection meaningfully interesting. Rendered in simple language and mostly free verse, they are sincere, full of emotion and filled with vivid imagery that will readily capture the attention of any reader.

Onyeali's "The Dowry of the Virgin" resonates with passion, promise and purpose, and will definitely appeal to lovers of poetry.

Dr. Margaret Fafa Nutsukpo
Department of English Studies
University of Port Harcourt
Port Harcourt, Nigeria

TABLE OF CONTENTS

UNPATRIOTIC COMMUNIQUE

I hate this robe I was found in
I wish I were found
Wearing a two-piece suit
With my nose shaped
Like the beak of the sword-fish
In a weak fish trap
This linen cloth I was girded with
Makes me poised
Like a bondsman
On God's swollen foot
I'd rather wear a birthday robe
Than to wear this piece of linen

I hate this place I was found in
I wish I were found
Strolling down to somewhere
And skyscrapers, penthouses
Fix their eyes upon me
I wish I were found in snow
And with a pipe between my lips
This sun melts me like wax

This thatched roof house
Makes me poised
Like a cat-fish on dry soil
I'd rather sail on a wavy sea
Than to live in this threshold

First published in Sunday Tide Newspaper on
the 15th of November, 1987

ANY WOMAN SCORNED

Oh, mighty wind!
What says your name?
Did you say Ikukuoma?
What a misnomer you have become!
That name is for angels
Are you angelic?
From your several deeds
I have known your trademarks
To brand you with a name mark
Fitting as a fiddle
You are no angel
But a broken wind

At your outbursts
Sailors are casted overboard
At the loss of your fiery temper
Sailors are buried in a twinkle
In the womb of the deep
Amidst claps of thunder
And sounds of fury

Indeed, Hell has no fury
Like a woman scorned

You are the windy tempest
That uprooted the old Iroko
Which you bestrode in a trice
For all to behold and fear
You conspired with your twin sister
That gentle breeze
Whom you coerced
To rid her gentleness
At the altar of your passion
Your proud father; sad old Tornado
Would kiss your angry lips
When you come home to roost

21st July, 2007

THE ELEPHANT'S STRIKES

From the green fields of war
Where weapons of warfare
Are briskly carnalised
Beyond enemy lines
Where strikes against enemy strikes
Are the ground rules of engagement
Behold, spoils of war are settled
In the bristling net
As shoals of herring are sorted out
From the fishing net

When push comes to shove
The Elephant brooks no retreat
Until conquest is carved out
From the lips of the umpire
Who runs about the battle-field
With a rule of the thumb
And a whistle in the mouth

Poised to corner for keeps
The second spoils of war

The Elephant shoots its last strikes
With a force of its first strikes
Behold Etoile has kissed the dust
Now the dust has settled at dusk

Let their dull hearts be engraved
On this stone of reminiscence
That this Elephant's triumph
Has stamped out twice
Their residue of shame
Hung on their stiff-necked
Like the Rock of Gibraltar.

In December, 2004
In remembrance of Enyimba's Victory over
Etoile in Caf championship league

THE MIDNIGHT CHILDREN

In this black and darkest night
When solemn hearts have gone numb
Masked faces with mascara
Are seen with manicured claws
And pedicured ten toes
They are talking wild in violet steps
And skyscraper heels
Marching down the market square
In search of their soul-mates
For the sales of God's temples

In the pitch dark they are
Some footfalls advance
Towards them like thuds
Their soul-mates are here
Knowing what to give
And what to take in return
Like lambs led to the slaughter's house
Off they follow to the wild side
Where they lose their fouled souls

Eating soured grapes hidden
Under their skimpy roses.

In the pitched dark they are
Other footfalls appear
Mightier than their soul-mates by far
Their missions interred with their deeds
Which in their hearts
Are engraved as tales
Told their seeds to bewail
Boots and finger marks enshrined
On bodies like scratches from hell
Their peacock dresses are in shreds
As cries like their pleas go unheard

In the pitch dark they are
Other footfalls advance
Towards them like the wild
Seeking to take away their breath
But not their bread
That has turned ashes
In their mouths
As their freedom tonight of spell
Is not in their hands to take
Some nights too damp to cheer
With no breath enough to share

In the pitch dark they are
Falls like rains and pours
Skimpy roses drip with falls
Like drops from vultures

Bedraggled on twigs
Hands wrap bodies from chills
Too cold their hearts benumbed
To eavesdrop on the morning cry
But they are the midnight children
Whose only hope of redemption lies
On the scarlet thread that flies.
At the window's wall of Jericho.

On 22nd August, 2007

THE OMNIPOTENT CREED

Groping
Through the labyrinth
Of uncharted tunnel
Your solemn footfalls
Thud along mine
Like a lamp unto my feet
I see light that leads me
To the tunnel's end

Pining away
In a lonely cell
The labial sound
Of your mantra
Filters through my heart
Like a sunbeam on the wall
I see joy that groves my soul

Falling from grace
Into a miry clay
Your outstretched hands
Lift me up

To your bosom
Like the apple of your dear heart
I see love that washes me clean

Squatting low
On my bended knees
Stoking my hearth
Your sweet name
Filters through my earlobes
Like a whispering thud
I see grace fills my heart
Like the smoke that billows the sky

HAVE YOU SEEN WHO
MY HEART TICKS FOR?

Have you seen
Who my heart ticks for?
 Behold! She is like a tender leaf
Hidden on the dry slope
Of the Northern hills

A rosebud
Hedged in the midst
Of piercing thorns

And a prayer
That calms down
My frayed nerves
And beats small
My mountain rage

Have you seen
Who my heart ticks for?
Behold! She is like a golden eagle
That soars high

Into the blue sky
A sweet song
Chirped by tens
Of humming birds
At the dawn
Of the morning light

A lullaby
That soothes my lumbago
And lures my brows
 To slumbering sounds

Have you seen
Who my heart ticks for?
Behold! She is like a merchandize
Of many kinds
In her brisk hands
Is a basket of treasures
To pleasure without measures
Purchased along the highway of time
Her love is like coats of onion bulbs
Persevered the teargas of its dissects peeled
You will live to see
The innermost beauty,
Pre- served.

Have you seen
Who my heart ticks for?
Behold! She is like a mother
Of many parts
Speechless messages like sweet wine

Flow freely from her blue eyes
Upon my dry gaze
A fountain that flows
In the midst of the valley
Strangers are often lost
In the mix of her words,
Un- heard.

Behold, the one whom my heart ticks for
Sitting as the queen
Beside my royal stool.

2nd September, 2007

IROKO

Oh, time tested Iroko!
How is the mighty fallen!
Is this your Waterloo
Or the dawn of your greatness?
Ably paved out
By the rhythm of the ages
And hummed like the songs of sages?
Truly, the downfall of a man: it says:
Is not the end of his life
Wake up, Wake up, man
And carry your can with calm
Live by the sage that says:
The groan of the spirit is his balm

21st July 2007

RIVERS OF RED WINE

Sandwiched
And Stacked
Between the Synagogue
And Mosque
Are trees hewn down in primes and kinds
Along the streets of Samarkand.
Out of their bellies
Flowed like ferries
Rivers of Red wine
Upon the face of this Riverine.

Banquets of red wine for the earth soil
All brewed in fits and turmoil
And so did the earth open its mouth wide
To drink some deluge of red tide
And got poisoned with bellyache
Just like new wine broke old wine rack
And spilled
The earth soil spewed
Out red wine in a pool
Upon the face of the earth like a fool.

Surfeit of red wine for the earth soil
None brewed for the sons of the soil
To wet the lips parched by the scene
Only the earth's vomit is seen
Which is not the Lord's brew
But the wine brewed by the Serpent's crew
Bedraggling the earth like the morning's dew.

On the 27th October, 2007

WHEN HE SEES HIS FRIEND
TURNS FOE

His hopes fall freely
Like dead leaves fall from treetops
In a whirlwind
His heart tumbles in turmoil
Like trapped soul in hurricane's grip
When he sees his friend turns foe

His eyes bulge out to flee
Like a bird before the scarecrow
In the vineyard
His lips glue to his tongue
Like a wax upon a jar's lid
When he sees his friend turns foe

His head looms larger
Like a balloon rising to burst
In the blue sky
His body trembles and shivers
Like debris in a whirlwind
When he sees his friend turns foe

His hands string the stringed unseen
Like a bondsman before his master's gong
In the manor
His legs are heavily laden in bond
Like a milestone on him that drowns
When he sees his friend turns foe.

8th December, 2007

ODE TO A FIEND

Many years have flowed by
Like the old blue River Nile
Passing through the long miles
Since you engraved yourself
With this festering wound
Made sore by ubiquitous,
Stubborn flies; whose ears
Are embedded on the ground:
Having hands writing tabloids
With fabled twist
And mandibles
Eating away flesh,
Souls and mind
With avaricious speed
Of the angry gods
Feasting on the accursed bread
Of the unholy sacrament

Who can but mend his wounds?
None but him
Can undo what's been long done

In his life next
For today's volte-face has evaporated
Into the transcendental plane
Like steam in the tropical sun
Where eyes can see but darkly
Man of political juggernaut!
Descend into your abyss; obey your Karma
From your fantasized lofty heights
Yield your mangled soul
To the waiting arms of your lonely mound
As you slumber at the place of your rest
Mankind has reached his place of rest
Adieu, my fiend of the people.

3rd February, 2008

WHERE HAVE OUR FATHERS GONE?

On this terrestrial stage
We will stand
To sing and dance our parts
Before our unseen celestial beings
But where have our fathers gone?
Who did shed their skin for us
Is it our will or a will foretold?
They have left us to our fate
But not with empty-handed faith
But with songs and dance steps to rhyme
And cast us through the stage of our time

Poised to perform with glee
In our fathers' figured footsteps
Our feet are heavily laden in pain
As our voices are drowned in droves
By the deafening sound of their doom
Overwhelmed with stage fright we stare
We cannot throw our first steps straight

Nor open our clipped lips with ease
To chant songs buried in our hearts
Which our feet can hardly interpret

But dance and sing we must
This is our fate not a curse
We cannot retreat and bloom
Nor stagnates like tree trunks
Brooding on their decamp for long
Lest the floodlight cast us wrong
Or show our cowardice feet numb
Before our celestial beings unseen
Whose wraths we can incur on the scene
But whose screams we cannot withstand.
In their streams

Our fate is cast on the stone
For our fathers have all stowed
Through the backstage of the world
Away to higher stage calls to obey
In quest for new songs and dance steps
Unto us will they solely bequeath
On ascension to the stage above
When our bells shall toll for us
The mantle of our carriage shall fall
On our seeds that blare our stead.

3rd February, 2008

DEAR BARACK, SON OF OBAMA

In the city of white beaches
A new star was seen
Riding upon the stallion's back
His sparkling eyes were found
Fastened upon the throne
Sitting within the whitewall

Out of his mouth flows
Words of true change
From Washington's rhetoric
To the days of our dreams
A change we can believe in
Oh yes we can; yes we can

Unto him were shouts of chants
Weaving across the land
Barack! Barack! Son of Obama
Your kingdom has come
On the doorsteps of our morning sun
Please preside for peace

Enemies reformed,
Old hatchets buried
In the sand of time
Upon chewed words at roundtables
Where unwitting elders tread not
Whose missiles suck innocents' blood
Which ricochet off the enemy's wall
To rebound upon the homeland
As putrefying incense
Hanging in the air
Like the swords of Damocles

You are neither white nor black
But a velvet voice for the voiceless pop
You are neither pope nor Imam
But a beacon of hope for the hoi polloi
Through the labyrinth of uncharted tunnel
Kennedy's reborn on the threshold
Of our slumbered hearts

He who crosses the Rubicon
Cast not his glare backward
On bated breath
Lest he stagnant
Like a pillar of salt
Arise like the morning sun
And wipe the bleeding
Eyes of the world
Duty calls; Whitehouse beckons;
You'll obey

At the going down of the sun
Your marks will meet
At the nick of time
For your darts are thrust
From the depth of your heart

6th March, 2008

THE SAIL OF OUR
TWISTED MASTERS

They said they are sailing
To a land far from our shores
In search of the opium
For the tares of our land
Another tale by moonlight

Now they have sailed
With our goodly pearls
Mined from pots that leaks
Which they have spread
At every port of call

Some fell by the way side
Others on fallow grounds
Where candles lit paved streets
And flowers sprang with kinds
All watered with our sweats

They muzzle us like Oxen
Hurling curfews on our heels

To keep us away from our pots
Which they kept with their kinds
Until they'll return

Now they have sailed
Back to our shorelines
With basketful of bangs
That Split our earlobes in two
While our masters probe not

Here they gathered us to see
Bridges across to no sea
Night sleeps too many nights
And highways of no return
Yet they bid us to keep
This fire burning still.

12th November, 2008

IN THE LAND NOT FAR FROM HERE

In the land not from here
The voices of the people
Like the songs of frogs
Are always muffled
With clipped ears
By those who sit on thrones
And make their kinds
Tumbling footstools

But as darkness falls
Upon the land
They grope through the dark
Like termites crawling
Into ram-shackle holes

But before their eyes
Pebbles of all kinds
Like patters of raindrops
Are hurled upon their roofs
From their neighbors' glass house
Built with waters
Drawn from the wells

Amidst the pestilence
They trudge down
To Saint Peter's Square
Like ants filing
Out of its besieged hills
To recite the Holy creeds
For answers long rendered
Before the foundation
Of their words

Before their eyes
Tongues of roaring fire
Dot the skylines
Like clustered bombs
Sucking dry the dark wells
Hidden in God's swollen foot
For the latter rains
But their feet are seen
Walking down the wild side
Like heavy hearts burdened
Under the spell of wine
Their voices are heard
Humming cords of fairy tales
That the skyline blues
Will wash away
With the tides of time

5th December, 2008

THE SUPREME LIES

What have you all gone out to see
Within the king's courtyard?

Brood of flowers
Shaken with the wind
Whose falling leaves
Subvert man's will
And send shivers
And dark clouds
Across our home land?

Or horde of trees and timber
Whose budding buds are plucked up
Before they'll grow
To bear fruits of goodly vine
Flourishing like River Nile
Across our home land?

Whose reports shall we then believe?
Those of the staring eyes
From far and near

Standing by the polls?
Or the grey-haired Daniels
Who did turn blind eyes
And deaf ears as spell cast
To the shrill cries of man?

Have they not planted a seal
Around a whirlpool of lies?
That bore rotten fruits on twigs
Upon which the culprits have sprung
Into tainted palaces
While the victims were repelled
From dimmed paradise.

Behold the hope of mankind dies!
When the fountain of justice dries
The lip of the nation cries
Under the weight of supreme lies
In this land, Daniels do not come to justice
But justice does come to Daniels
At twilight.

10th January, 2009

THE DOWRY OF THE VIRGIN

What cruel fate has befallen her?
Whom God has arrayed from birth
With fragrant scents of Hibiscus
Which spreads abroad on eagles' wings
Like the scent marks for the sharks
Attracting suitors of diverse kinds
From every corner of mankind
They came to tear and wear
Every flesh with avaricious speed

Behold, Virgin Delta has fallen
Into the hands of suitors of all kinds
Under the subtle touch of cold love
Made with sugar coated tongues
She was the candle of bright light
But they bruised the teats of her virginal glands
And polluted her body with bloody pool
Like the over-flow of the River Nile

They take away everything foretold
Her precious stones, pearls and gold

Hidden deep beneath her ebony skin
All gone like vapour in the tropical sun
Up they stand a long way off her shores
So rich with the wealth of Delta's stores
While she is left in ashes of ruins
Like an orphan child in a blistering cold

They broke this subtle of cold love
Made with sugar coated tongue
To secure the buds of Delta love
When the grasses were green
And the womb fertile like the Soil
Before the eclipse of the sun
By these suitors of divers rout
Like earth haggard to eons of drought.

Arise and pursue with gazelle's feet
These runaway bands of renegade breeds
And bring them back to Delta's shores
To obtain the full dowry of the virgin vowed
Or have them marry whom they deflowered
In the circle of the candlelight vigil
They lit this lamp of love like moon
So cannot run away from Delta's doom.

6th February, 2009

THE PREACHER

Let the sun shine wide-eyed
Or die in eclipse

Let the rains fall like showers
Or blown away by northerly wind

Let the stars twinkle like pearls of dews
Or crash to the earth's ravenous crush

Let the rivers flow into channels like joy
Or be swallowed by a sea of thirsty soil

Let the sands of Sahara wail like storm
Or sit in silence as the rock of ages.

Let the moon glow like the bloom of flowers
Or be covered under the bushel of the night

Let the sea rage like a woman scorned
Or calm its nerves like a solitary pond.

Let the wind blow like tales by moonlight
Or hold its breath like dead man's bones

Let the forest spring forth like Brazilian hairs
Or made bare by a blazing fire

Let the mountains tower like trees of hope
Or become piles of anthills of the Savannah.

Let the valleys carry river like hand basins
Or clasp together by mountainous rage

Let the night break forth into day like flood
Or die from nightmares of everlasting nights

Let the earth calm the ocean like a lullaby
Or be swallowed by the deep in a fit of rage

Let the air breathe life like water.
Or be choked by dark chimney's smoke

Let the sky dot stars like diamonds
Or be rolled away like a scroll by God's hands.

29th June, 2009

THE KIDNAPPERS

Sounds of gun shots like thunder
Drown the ubiquitous cries
Of his innocence
Staccato cries of scared faces
At the crossroads
Sounded like a wailing song
For this departing soul
Even here and now he still cries
Only if you can hear his whispering voice
Or the echoes of his far away drumbeats
Beckoning on you to set him free

Let your trigger happy lads
Lay down their weapons of fortune
Let them dip their heads low
In this crystal running water
Like the baptized of a true God
They can emerge with contrite hearts
Enough to keep the fireworks out of the sky
Or kill the euphoria that heralds his coming

Lest they kill the innocent soul
Of this orphaned child

He is not he whom you seek to find
Behold he sits atop the palace
With long robes and oiled fingers
Where he tramples upon
The letters of credence
With his right hand of falsehood
Which letters he sealed
With sugar coated tongues
Only to turn aside
To build for himself castles
Which like trees, touch the skylines
With the fruits of the vineyards
Ripe for all

He knows how deep and wide you have dug
Like a good tiller of the ground
You have dug for a good yield
He knows the pains of your foot sores
Which you seared from long treks
Of uncharted forest
Did he not hear
The cracks of your hipbones
While you ascended the eight hills
And trekked the ninth mile
Remember, he did plant his footmarks
On your baobab prints
As you led along the thorny paths

Grieve not my friends
Over how your enterprise may blossom
Like these tender buds of Hibiscus
The echoes of your ransom
Have resonated like whirlwind
And you still say it is life for a life
What I have will I give
For the soul
If he stays alive and serves his time
I shall have paid your ransom in kind

3rd September, 2009

THE RULER AND THE LEADER

There goes the ruler
Behind his sheep
Higher he soars
Like the stars of the sky
He is but a meteorite
With aimless ride
See how he leads his sheep
To stormy hails
Where a sea of heads
Have rotted to the skulls.

There he goes to and fro
His kingdom lane
Where he craves their love
With whips and chains
So strong and firm
Like the Afghan's will
When he withers like all men do
He is rafted
With the filth of his lonely grave

There goes the leader
Before his sheep
He is a star
Of the high blue sky
He sets his lamp alight
Which they follow
And leads them by
The banks of the shallow river
Where pastures are green
And tender low

There he goes to and fro
His kingdom lane
Where he craves their love
With a reed of staff
So strong and firm
Like a mother's love
When he withers
Like all men do
Rose petals spring up
By his beehive grave.

9th September, 2009

TREES AND FLOWERS

Trees are men.
Baobabs, Oaks,
Cedars and others
Are trees of life
Like the Garden of Eden.
Who can stand
The stems of Baobabs?
Who can stand
The forest of Oaks?
Who can stand
The trunks of Cedars?
It is only the strongest
That dares the jungle.
Birds of the air
Perch on their twigs
Singing songs of lullaby.
But out of their falls
Come a living shed
That serves us a roof
Over our heads

Flowers are women.
Roses, Hibiscus,
Chrysanthemum and others
Are lilies of life like ballads.
Who can stand
The kisses of Roses?
Who can stand
The tenderness of Hibiscus?
Who can stand
The fragrance of Chrysanthemum?
It is only the saints
That sees paradise
On the pollen
Birds of the air peck
Peck! Peck! Peck!
They fertilize the ovaries.
And thrive like a candle
In the wind
But out of their bellies
Come a thriving spring
That replenishes the world.

15th September, 2009

ONE NIGHT WITH THE KING

In my black and darkest night
Was I ushered before the Knight
Like one whose palm kernels
Were cracked
By his benevolent spirits
Lo, I beheld the king
Seated on his throne
Like the statue of Gad

Soon he stepped down
With girded steps
And led me to his banquet wine
Like an heir is led to his bride
From aisle to the altar

But as I settled down to duel
In the night's drink of spell
Sights of terror like flaming swords bewailed me
Betwixt and amidst his August assembly

Were eyes stabbing me
Like arrows of steel

Some were the lords of the highways
Like brood of Hyenas
Foraging the plains
Some were bitter tongues
Like hallowed portals of ruins
Some were hands dripping red wine
Which anointed Kingdom's paths
Some were feet
Swift to leave trails of wails
In their wakes
Some put price-tags on foreheads
And reaped baobab fruits
Others were lords
That removed landmarks
And became sorrows of dead men

Soon the King bestrode
The table wine
Like a colossus
While his lords wet
His outstretched hand
With kisses of lip love
And obeyed his mantra
Like the Sicilian god

The sights stabbed me
Like many arrows

And my heart bled
For a freedom flight
Soon his hand was mine to kiss
And the king beckoned
With his brown eyes on me

I fled his presence like a bird
From a fowler raged
Into the warm arms
Of a starless night
Where mortal eyes
Groped not my silent falls
Good night my king
Was all I could whisper
In my breathless speed
And may your Kingdom fall
Like a dead leaf
Was all my heart could beat
In staccato crescendo

One night with the king
Is like a thousand day
In the eyes of the blind

18th September, 2009

THE BLUES OF GAZA

Gaza is fallen! Gaza is fallen!
Like a dead leaf from a living branch
Into the hands of his beleaguered fathers

One litters the sky with fireflies
Which he calls from the pleasant land
Like Hyena's calls for a Tiger's dance
Fires are falling down like showers
Straight from the sky and city towers
Burning the city like wild fire
While he does nothing but cry
Crying a river like the crocodile
This hardly cleanses the blood flow
That anoints the streets of Gaza Strip

The other scrambles for the crumbs
That falls from the master's table
He sends heavy hearts to burrow
Highways of tunnels to the land of the Nile
Like a brood of moles rustling their nests

To and fro the dark holes
Are knees like ants that crawl
Back and forth and betwixt
They pull carts of sorts for the belly
And firewood to keep the fire still

Who can deliver this city
From the last jots of its blood
Which their fathers are poised to shed
As their lives' cords are put to shreds
Who can rid its gates of strong men
Who like Samson fight to keep the homeland
From angel lovers that burst like thunders
Who can deliver this city like Delilah
Whose charms melted the lion's heart
Whom she led to captive like a shearer's lamb

Gaza shall rise! Gaza shall rise!
Like a leaf of the living branch in the spring time
By the hands of his fathers of the latter rain.

On the 13th October, 2009

AFRICAN CHILD WITCHES

Samantha is a witch
So says the seer
Who's there to tell smeary tales
That throws a child
Away to the streets
Like a wandering star
Of the lonely night

But she was a rose
In the midst of thorns
Before this seer
Fixed her with horns
Which she carries about
With dread locks
Like a rose flower
Tottering on the rocks

She went to school
Behind the shadows
Of eyebrows raised
Like the owls

Before she was baptized
In the rains
Lest she brush them
With tar of witchery

She lurks around the square
Like overnight log
Where lucky lips
Read her ribs like numbers
But her beleaguered eyes
Only read lip's bound hands
Like a beggar's gaze
Upon empty palms

One day her angel's tears
Fell like raindrops
On God's footstool
And made a pool of light
Shinning brighter than the stars
All around her
Telltale's signs of sorrows depart
Beyond the seas
That any eyes could see
Her witchery flames

Uwem is a witch
So says the seer
Who's there to tell smeary tales
That makes the mother's love
Grow cold like the wind
Of Jos Plateau

She needs a healing
So says the seer
Unlike the tenderness
Of her mother's touch
Whose grace flows like a river
In the warm arms
That rocks the cradle

She is remorseless
So says the Seer
Whose seed of mercy
Is like a dried bone
Which only God knows
If it will rise again
From the ashes of his swollen foot
To the hope of her timeless reigns

Up to the hills
She took her child
Like Mary's boy child
Jesus Christ led to hide
Betwixt ends she shuffles
To relieve the cords
Of a suckling child

Mama, mama
She calls out in pains
To any mother
That meets her eyes
But her wrinkled face
Tells her tales

From her cradle
To the land of her deport

Malinze is a wizard
So says the Seer
Who's there to tell smeary tales
He casts a spell
Upon this poor child
With nine inches longish nail

He screams now
Like a rabid soul
A lost mind who can bear
Except the saints
Who like the stars
Can lighten up
His ghostly face

He was cast
Into the firestorm
Like a piece of metal
Forged in the furnace
Now he is charred
And walks like zombies
Whose only solace
Is the cover of the night

He was hungry
But fed with pebbles
Which shape his teeth
Like vampire's canines

He was decked
In a hangman's noose
To snuff the witchery flame
Out of his life

His head was carved
Like Halloween bust
Which they steadied
On God's swollen foot
He drank the poison like gravy
Yet he lives to tell
The tales of his sorrows

6th November, 2009

FAIR HAVENS

The white man's moon
Tunnels nigh
From the eyes
Of the hall of silence
Upon this brazen candle
It dwells
Where moths
And butterflies go aflame
And cast off
On the monument of time
Upon which stood
This sumptuous ruby
Who being un-spoilt
But too disfigured
To the humming of the song master
He is now sandwiched
In the trees of hope
Though transparent,
And too naked
To be holier than his gallant fronts

His lips shiver
Like parched leaves in the harmattan
His heart ripples in turmoil
And entangles
In the ghostly web of the spider
Now, he has become
A suckling child
Some spirited speeches
Have turned ashes in his mouth
But the die is cast,
Says; the song master
I am the expectant mother
You, the dutiful midwife
 Mark me deeper
With the sharp dagger of your pupil

If I were to be your robes
Would I not dine
Where angels dare not?
But you sleep
Deeper than the deep
Are you a log of wood?
Sprinkled ashes
Do nothing to the ancient satyr
But you are a spirit;
Catwalk is your trademark
Please, what time
Does the thunder bolt strike?
Act! Act! Act!
Time is but a mischievous lover

Oh! How the stream of time flows
With the frosty wind that blows
The angelic facade
To and fro in crescendo.

Sometime in 1991 in the University

THE SONGS OF
THE METALLIC GRASSHOPPERS

Come to me
All you kindred spirits
Ride with me
On the fast and furious lanes
Let's ride
Swifter than Cheetahs
Could on the plains
But while we ride
On the road's twists
And turns
Shine your eyes
Like the sun's wide eye
In a cloudless sky
For you may never see
Eye to eye
The deep loop
Of your going
And coming

Wherein you may meet
Your waterloo

Ride with me,
All you kindred spirits
Off we go
On an endless ride
Like the meteorites
Ride to collide
Or roam to and fro
The darkling planes
Where we will stare
The sun ball's eye
And wrestle
The rains railing rage
And live to tell
The tales of the sages
Before the dawn
Of our twilights

Turn aside
All you kindred spirits
Crawl with your bruised heels
And broken hands
Like a toddler
On the tumbling crèche.
That is but one fairy tale
We'll pay for our wild
And aimless ride

In strength and weakness rife
We'll ride through this storm
To the land in distance
Of no return

16th July, 2012

ASHES OF RUINS

On the city slope
Of the sleepy Niger
Just like the cities
Of its kindred spirits
Hurrying feet are gathering
Like the ants
Of the anthills of Savannah
On this broken land.
Just like a bird to a snare,
Knowing not
It is life for a life
Behold a sea has broken forth
Like a flood
But the hope of the sea
Is like a broken dream

The People's hearts
Are already broken in pieces
As the spirit of lust
Is cast upon the tearful Tank
Whose heart is broken in two,

Like the old rusted pipes
Rested before now
In wild and reckless abandonment
Behold, it is bleeding profusely
Like Moses' rock
Gutting forth
Like a healing stream
Though prostrated
Yet castrated in seductive poise
To satisfy the old orgies
Of man long denied

Behold, Sea of hungry heads
Lock panting horns
In discordant voices
Of disagreed tones
Kindred spirits
Entangling in the web
Of a burning love
But only the fittest of the fittest
Copulate here in wild ecstasy
They are ejaculating now,
But striking different notes
Of multiple orgasm
Prostrated Tank like old Pipes
Could no longer hold
But bleed fumes of fury
Like gang-raped harlots.

Soon the flame of love
Gives way to wild fire,

Flame of fire burning
Ala staccato in crescendo
Like thunder-bolts strike in turmoil
Behold, the pride,
And the beauty of Niger
Are engulfed
In the inferno of ecstasy
Now, charred
But walking zombies
Like jilted lovers are littered
In the streets of Niger
Like a thousand Juliet
And Romeo in poisoned chalice

The voices of mothers are heard
Like a sounding brass
But the faces of their children
Dim like echoes of distant drums
The walking dead
Are dropping on footpaths
Like rotten grapes from twigs.
The sick bay bedraggles
With blood overflow
Crying mothers cry more
Because the voices of their children
Remain silent in interlude
Like the stars of the silent screens

These flowing tears
Of kindred spirits
Pour down

Like rains of Amazon forest
But not enough
To quench the fury of fire
That tears apart
The souls of innocent children
Who, before now,
Were the trees of this land

Behold, the dreams of the fallen stars
Are broken apart
Like dead leaves from twigs
And shall rise no more
From the ashes of ruins

27th July, 2012

COCKCROW AT DAWN

The darkest night melted
Beyond the throes
Of the besieging dawn
Like a veil of mist
Unfurled in the sky
But from the bamboo bed
I depended
I did not accept
It was late for lying
Though, the sun was uprising
From slumber
Like one refusing
To give up a brawl
Of the night before

But clearly I heard
The sound of the cockcrow
Cringing upon my earlobes
Like the sound of a wake-up call
But the distinct sound I heard
Was not the sound of conquest

Nor was it of vanquished
But the sound of war
Beckoning on me
To prepare for the war-front
That besieged me
Like the swords of Damocles

But my heart was torn in two
When the swords of light
Tunneled in for a duel
Through the cracks slit open
By the bullets of the twin brothers
Littered with unfeigned fate
From the belly of the lioness
But my fear was hidden
Behind the veils of my cringing brows
Like a lily-livered soldier
Cornered by a battle-wizened general

Behind the walls
Were the footfalls
Of some beleaguered soldiers
Treading down to the frontlines
To lock horns
With the day's armies of pain

Down trodden to the river
The children dropped down pots
Down trodden to the square
The mothers dropped down baskets
Down trodden to the forests

The men dropped down hoes
Down trodden to the door
I stood with my breastplate
To behold the morning sun
And still lived beyond the sunset.

04th September, 2013

THE BALLAD IN THE DESERT

Memories
Are like moving pictures
But only silence can see
The scenes unfold
And in the mind's eye
Does it construct.

Just like the old fabled wine
Turned from the Jar of water
Was divine
The days of my pilgrimage
Have swiftly broken before me
From dawn to twilight
Like a flash of lightning

It was just but yesterday
I took my first steps forward
Under my mother's gaze
To scribble with my peers
Unlettered words of infant's mind
On the sand of time

Which words I first muttered
Under my breath.
Like a tongue-twister
On a roller-coaster

But upon the break
Of a new dawn
I found myself no longer
A suckling child
But a mouthpiece
Chewing round words
In a round mouth
In the land of my birth
Until twin tongues
Became daggers' drawn
Upon my loquacious lips
One was my mother's tongue
The other
The tongue of a stranger
Which stood before me
Like a colossus
Without which
I could neither buy nor sell
In the land of my birth

Behold my mother's tongue
Have I lost
Groping for the one
Of the distant land
For which I am still tottering
At my wit's end

We will sit there
Under the moonlight
Like a gathering brood
There we bared
Our earlobes to hear
Fairy tales of wonder lands
Under the prying eyes
Of a thousand stars
That dotted the skylines
Like a diamond's sparks

Upon the crevices
Of a thousand hills
We stooped over the cliffs
On our steady heels
Upon which I casted
My first hooks in the deep
Behold my hooks
Were as slippery as the fishes
But after many plunges
In stirred waters
I did catch some little breeds
Who will keep me
From dying no more
When they shall tell the tales
Of my heroes past

Upon the stage of my crafts
I walked the lines
Of multi-coloured scripts
From one stage of sublime

To the absurd of sobs
For which I reached out
To tinker betwixt
And between
To agree with today's beats
But my arm was too short
To wipe the indelible marks
In the sky
Which my eyes
Could behold but darkly
Behold my deeds
Have come before me
Like the imprints
Of scattered footsteps
Left behind on the sand of time
Though they lived so far
In the dim past
There is always a chord
Line of trace
That lurks behind me
Like a shadow ray.

The moon wrapped
Her arms around me
Like a cascade of shade
Upon the horizon
As my journey drew close
To begin anew
I opened my eyes
To close the eyes of my mind
Which borne me

Upon the eagle's wings
Beyond the shores
Of the dim past
Where my feet
Dared not tread last
I casted my eyes
Upon the wind's drops
And I saw some eyes
Have dimmed low
Like sunset upon the horizons
While some rested their heads
On a lonely mound
Paved by the monument
Of silent image
That I cringed
But my fears soon faded
Into illuminating stars
Who heralded my welcome
From a journey so far

On the 11th January, 2013

THE ECLIPSE OF THE SUN

They are
In the world
But they are not
Of this world

For the world
In which they are
Is like the world of Zeus
Where the gong
Of the yonder land
Echoes on the shores
Of this land
Soothing upon their earlobes
Like a whispering thud

But as the sun rises
From the east
To set at dawn
In the West
Darkness falls

Upon the land
Like the plague
Of the land of the Nile

Beleaguered souls
Stagger thro' the halls
Like palm-wine drinkers run,
Groping in the labyrinth
Of the glistering sun

In crescendo
The sun blinks once in a while
With a twisted smile
Upon bodies swimming
In ocean deep sweats
Whose robes drench
In the sweats that pour
Like raindrops
Behind the walls

Like the sun before it
The moon blinks
Its eye a thousand times
Like the fireflies
At night calls
Ushering the footfalls
Of unholy wedlock
Of fair-weather friends
Flocking together
In harmony

Behold, starry eyes
Tiptoeing with clayed feet
Leap over the walls
Of eyes of deep sleep

Alas, metallic voices
Are heard
From the eerie sound
That emits
Splitting earlobes
Like a sounding brass
And hearts wake
From slumbering snores

Sparks of lights
Are seen for a time
Sneezing fumes
On the horizon fronts
Hurrying feet walk
On the wild side
Like the castaways trudge
On the walk side
Leaving the land
To fallow hearts
Like the Sabbaths
Of the Holy Land.

Lo, upon the blink
Of an eyelid
Shouts of the battle cry

Break loose upon them
Like the rush
Of a mighty flood
They must either expire
Like lilies before their time
Or live to fight another day
Like the spring
Of the tender buds of Violet
Before the sunrise

This sun, I say, must not eclipse,
A second time

26th August, 2013

BROKEN EGG

Tender-hearted
Like budding bud
Pants after stony grounds
Like panther pants after water

Lily-hearted
Like water reeds
Shakes in turmoil
Like candle in the wind

Violet blue
Like tremor
Thrives in the wild
Like debris in whirlwind

Bitter words
Like many arrows
Pierce the heart
Like broken egg

Heart bleeds like spilt milk
On God's mending ground

10th September, 2013

Review Requested:

If you loved this book, would you please
provide a review at Amazon.com?

Lightning Source UK Ltd.
Milton Keynes UK
UKHW011830260620
365625UK00001B/109